Making Movies

by Annie Buckley

The Child's World®
www.childsworld.com

Published in the United States of America by The Child's World®
P.O. Box 326 • Chanhassen, MN 55317-0326
800-599-READ • www.childsworld.com

ACKNOWLEDGMENTS

The Child's World®: Mary Berendes, Publishing Director

Produced by Shoreline Publishing Group LLC
President / Editorial Director: James Buckley, Jr.
Designer: Tom Carling, carlingdesign.com
Cover Art: Slimfilms
Copy Editor: Beth Adelman

Photo Credits:
Cover—Getty Images (Main); Corbis (insets).
Interior—AP/Wide World: 9, 16, 20; Corbis: 4, 7, 11, 12, 13, 15, 17, 27;
Getty Images: 19, 23, 28; Rex USA: 8, 25.

LIBRARY OF CONGRESS CATALOGING-IN-PUBLICATION DATA

Buckley, Annie.
  Making movies / by Annie Buckley.
     p. cm. — (Girls rock!)
  Includes bibliographical references and index.
  ISBN 1-59296-746-9 (lib. bound : alk. paper)
 1. Motion pictures—Juvenile literature. 2. Cinematography—
Juvenile literature. I. Title. II. Series.
  PN1994.5.B83 2006
  791.43—dc22
                        2006001643

CONTENTS

GET READY TO
Film

Did you ever wonder how movies are made? It's a lot of work! A movie that's only two hours long might take months or even years to make.

Making movies involves more than just the actors. It takes a team of creative, skilled people. Even if you only see one actor on the screen, you're watching the work of hundreds of people.

So, when people are going to make a movie, where do they start?

A movie starts with an idea for a story. This can come from the writer, the **producer**, the **director**, even the **movie studio**. A writer then creates a *screenplay*, which is the entire story of the movie, including all the words the actors will say.

The producer is basically in charge of planning the movie, including finding money to pay for it. The director is in charge of the actual filming.

Like all good writing, the screenplay goes through many changes before it is ready to be filmed. Once the screenplay is finished, the studio puts together the group of actors (the *cast*).

The rest of the filmmaking team is put together, too. That might include hundreds of people! Then, the people in charge decide where the movie will be filmed.

Choosing the actors for a film is called "casting." The filmmakers use video to help make their choices.

This set was built for the French film Babette's Feast. *It was made to look like the 1890s.*

Parts of many movies—and sometimes whole movies—are filmed on **sets**. Sets are specially built to look like towns, houses, spaceships, other planets, or anything else you can imagine!

Unlike real buildings, sets aren't meant to last for many years. Instead, they're built with lightweight materials such as plastic and wood. Many of the walls and doors you see in movies have nothing on the other side.

Here's a shot of Hobbiton, from the Lord of the Rings movies. The house has been added, but the location is real—it's a field in New Zealand.

Some movies are filmed in real places—"on location." Finding the right locations can take moviemakers all over the world.

Deciding where to film each part of the movie and building the sets can take months. Planning and making costumes for the actors to wear can take months, too. Everything has to be just right!

Makeup is important, too. Bright lights are used in

Famous actor Gene Hackman poses with some of the super-bright lights used in moviemaking.

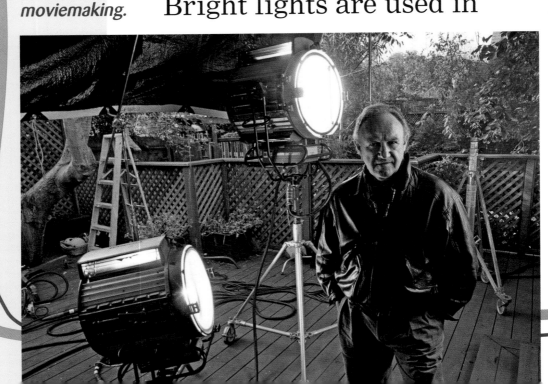

You wouldn't know it from seeing him on the screen, but French actor Guillaume Depardieu is wearing a lot of makeup!

filming. The lights mean that the actors must wear more makeup than anybody would in the real world. Makeup artists work their magic to turn actors into everything from beautiful princesses to frightening monsters.

The movie has been carefully planned, and now everyone gets ready to start filming.

Movies aren't filmed all at once. Instead, they're shot one part, or *scene*, at a time. The scenes don't have to be shot in order. Instead, they're filmed in whatever order works best. If some scenes need to be filmed in a different location, it's easier to shoot all at once than to travel back and forth!

The actors have done lots of

homework by the time filming begins. They've learned all about the characters they will play. They've learned the lines they must say and what they must do, and they've practiced their parts. Now, filming is about to start!

Director Susan Stroman is shown with a movie camera as she gets ready to start filming The Producers.

2

LIGHTS, CAMERA, Action!

The first step in filming is for filmmakers to decide exactly how they want to put the scene on film. Will the camera show the actors from a distance, or close up? Where will the camera be placed? Will it show the actors from the front or from the side? How will the scene be lit? A **cinematographer** works with the director to answer those questions.

Then the lights and camera need to be set up. Lighting is important for showing the time of day, the mood, and the actors' faces. Lights are needed even if it's supposed to be nighttime in the film. Getting the lights and camera set up can take a lot of time.

Actor Alexsei Chadov waits for cameras and lights to be set up on the set of the movie Serko.

To frame a shot, directors, such as Wim Wenders here, sometimes use their hands to help them picture what the camera will film.

Finally, the director calls for the actors to take their places. The director looks through the camera to see how everything will look on film. This is called "framing the shot." The edges of the film act like a picture frame. The director has lots of choices about what to show inside that frame.

Types of Shots

Choosing what picture to show often means choosing how the camera is pointed. The direction of the camera can change how a scene looks and feels. Some examples of different types of "angles" used to film a movie include:

- Reaction shot: the face of an actor is shown reacting to something that has happened.
- Close up: Only one actor's face takes up the entire shot. The top photo shows Johnny Depp in close up from the movie *Willy Wonka and the Chocolate Factory*.

- Long shot: The camera is far away from the actors.
- Wide shot: The camera captures more of a scene from side to side, often from farther away. A wide shot from *Willy Wonka* is the bottom picture.

Holding this slate in front of the camera when shooting begins helps everyone keep track of what's on the film. The slate shows the movie, the date, and the scene.

Just before actual shooting begins, the assistant director calls out, "Quiet on the set!" Everyone who's not acting—and there can be dozens of people on the set—must keep quiet while the film is rolling so that no extra sounds end up in the film.

When everything is ready, the director says "Action!" and the cameras start to roll. The actors speak their lines or perform actions. They continue to play their parts until the director says, "Cut!" That means to stop filming . . . and stop acting.

Some directors use video screens to watch filming.

Sometimes everything goes perfectly the first time, and the scene is filmed in one "take." Usually, actors use several—or many—takes to get the scene just right. Each time, the actors might say their lines a little differently or move in a different way.

The director gives them suggestions on what to change. Sometimes, the cinematographer might suggest something to change in the lights or angle. This part of moviemaking takes patience!

More and more takes are filmed. Lights are changed, different angles are used, the actors say their lines in different ways. Finally, everyone is satisfied and the scene is done. Now it's time to film the next scene . . . and then the next.

One very interesting part of some movie scenes is the work of *stunt* people. These experts take the place of actors when a scene calls for doing something that is possibly dangerous. Stunt people prepare carefully and are well trained. They might fall from a building, race a car, or jump through a window. It's all part of movie magic!

Take Five

Making a movie is fun, but it's also a lot of hard work! The cast and crew usually work long hours. They are often on the set for 16 or more hours a day. When they get breaks, a director might say "Everybody, take five," meaning five minutes. Because everyone is working so hard, the studio provides meals and snacks. Everyone eats together and rests between takes.

Superstar Jennifer Lopez takes a break between takes of Maid in Manhattan *to grab a quick snack on the set.*

3

IT'S A Wrap!

Filming a movie can take many months. The cast and crew might have to travel long distances to different locations. They might have to wait for just the right weather so they can film. Finally, though, all the filming is done—the movie is a **wrap**. The cast and film crew are finished with their work. Often, the studio throws a big party for everyone who helped with the filming.

The filming might be over, but the movie isn't finished yet. There's still a lot of work to do.

Sean Astin, Elijah Wood, Liv Tyler, Dominic Monaghan, Billy Boyd, and other cast and crew members from the Lord of the Rings *movies enjoy a party together.*

After the wrap, the *post-production* crew gets to work ("post-" means "after"). First, the **editor** and the director choose the best take for each scene. Then the scenes must be arranged in the right order to tell the story. Some scenes don't really add much to the story, and they are shortened or even cut out completely.

Then the **visual effects** team adds all the things that can't be filmed in real life. For example, they might use a computer to create a

monster or to add a background showing a scene from outer space. In many movies made today, these experts combine scenes filmed using real actors with scenes created on a computer.

You can't set real actors on fire! So how do you create an awesome character like the Human Torch in The Fantastic Four? *You use a computer.*

Besides visual effects, music and other sounds must be added to the film, too. And once the film is finished, dozens more people go to work to tell the world all about it.

The first night the movie is shown, there's often a big party called a **premiere** (preh-MEER). The stars come dressed in beautiful gowns or tuxedos. Everyone is excited to see how the film looks and whether people like it. Now you know all the hard work it took to reach this big day!

GLOSSARY

cinematographer   the person responsible for the lighting and camera work and the general look of a movie

director   the person responsible for making a movie

editor   the person who prepares the final version of a movie by deciding which takes and scenes to use

movie studio   a company that makes movies

premiere   the first public showing of a new movie

producer   the person who puts together the team of people who create a movie

sets   places, rooms, or buildings built just to film a movie

visual effects   special additions to the look of a movie that don't exist in real life

wrap   when the process of filming a movie is complete

FIND OUT MORE

BOOKS

*Attack of the Killer Video Book: Tips and Tricks
for Young Directors*
by Mark Shulman and Hazlitt Krog
(Annick Press, Toronto, Ontario) 2004
This all-in-one book helps YOU make your own movie!

Eyewitness: Film
by Richard Platt
(DK Publishing, New York) 2000
This book covers cameras, film, motion pictures, stars, studios,
makeup, props, special effects, and many other topics.

*Lights, Camera, Action!:
Making Movies and TV from the Inside Out*
by Lisa O'Brien
(Maple Tree Press, Toronto, Ontario) 1998
This book describes two teenagers auditioning for roles in a
film and then explains every step of how the film is made.

*Movie Science: 40 Mind-Expanding, Reality-Bending,
Starstruck Activities for Kids*
by Jim Wiese
(Jossey-Bass, Hoboken, NJ) 2001
This is a step-by-step look at how movies are made.

WEB SITES

Visit our home page for lots of links about movies and
moviemaking: www.childsworld.com/links

Note to Parents, Teachers, and Librarians: We routinely check our Web links to
make sure they're safe, active sites—so encourage your readers to check them out!

INDEX

Growing up in Los Angeles, **ANNIE BUCKLEY** was surrounded by Hollywood and movies. She remembers going to the Warner Brothers studio as a young girl to see a Western town that looked so real, she felt like Annie Oakley! Annie is the author and illustrator of the *The Kids' Yoga Deck*, coauthor of *Once Upon a Time: Creative Writing for Kids*, and author of three other Girls Rock! books. She thanks her husband, artist and filmmaker Dane Picard, for his helpful input on this book.